Wounded Butterfly

Wounded Butterfly

A Collection of Poetry, Prose, and Deep Thoughts by

Margie Watts

With Much Love ~ Margie Watts

INDEPENDENTLY PUBLISHED

i

Dedication

For all the Wounded Butterflies who still feel the darkness even in the light. Who still see the rain on a sunny day and feel lost and alone. You are not alone. Remember, the most beautiful souls bloom in the dark and the light isn't always scary.

Special Dedication

For Robert, you are the light in my darkness.
My children, Erin, Tiffany and John. Erin, U R My ❤. John and Tiffany, my sweet baby angels, may my love always reach you in heaven.
To Robin, you are and always will be my daughter.

Daddy don't cry, your Wounded Butterfly finally learned how to fly... I miss you, thank you for believing in me when no one else did. Sending so much love to you up in Heaven.

"But on paper, things can live forever. On paper, a butterfly never dies."
~ Jacqueline Woodson

Acknowledgements

To be honest, I actually researched the proper way to write an acknowledgement page. I studied the examples and who/what it should start with, blah, blah, blah. Anyone who truly knows me, well, you get it.

So...

With all my heart

I want to thank Jay Long for helping me realize some hearts are truly special. For taking the time to help me be proud of my accomplishment and turn my soul into what I truly envisioned it to be.

I want to thank Daniel Mercury at Daniel Mercury Designs who designed the beautiful cover for my soul. Daniel's design tells a story all within itself.

To all of the beautiful souls that have walked this journey with me, thank you. All of you have been a blessing. I only wish I could name each and every one of you, but you know who you are. You know I love you.

Last and by far not least

My Grandchildren: Erien, Aime, Tiana, Sydnie, and Greyson.

I hope one day when you are old enough to read Wounded Butterfly, you will remember who I became because of the darkness. I love you all.

Foreword

When I was first asked to edit Wounded Butterfly, I didn't know Margie Watts' story. Once I dove into the project, I immediately understood this was more than a book. This was a journey - her journey.

Each page is an unrestrained, and real portrayal of her life. The pain and uneasiness are palpable, but the hope and determination are truly felt. Margie's storytelling brings the reader right there with her. Some pieces are poetic, and others are completely raw. Either way, Margie's storytelling brings the reader right along with her through the tears, the pain, the fear, the hope, and the survival.

Wounded Butterfly is one woman's walk into, though, and out of Hell. By telling her story, Margie Watts has given a voice to those who are silent. Anyone who has experienced abuse will finally say, "I'm not alone." Anyone who can't imagine the toll abuse takes on someone will better understand just how devastating it can be because of Margie's story.

Jay Long
February 2020

Preface

When I decided to put Wounded Butterfly together, I wasn't
sure how my unconventional way of writing would be
received. Most of us read poetry and books like this about
love and the beauty of life. I write about the dark side of love
and life. Sometimes it's raw but it is from my soul. These
pages contain pieces of me. I write about the physical and
emotional abuse of love. Sadly, I write about the secret life
behind closed doors. The secrets no-one talked about when I
was growing up or when I was a wife. Times have changed, it
is still happening but now it is talked about. There are far too
many victims out there suffering in silence. This is my way of
giving them a voice.

So, I'm not putting my writings together as just a story of
survival. This is part of my healing, my process, part of my
journey.
--

Margie Watts

Introduction

Wounded Butterfly is my journey out of the "Dark Night" of my Soul. A journey back into the light and the strength it took to see it through to the end.

Wounded Butterfly was my life, for lack of a better description. I try to reach outside of myself to seek the answers I need to aide me through the healing process. I also try to remember that everyone has their journey in life, and it is up to each of us to be a blessing to those we touch. Everyone has a story and my story is no more important than yours. Everyone is worthy, unique, and special. It is not up to anyone to judge me or others. Pain is pain, and it fucking (pardon the f bomb) hurts.

"There can be no rebirth without a dark night of the soul, a total annihilation of all that you believed in and thought that you were."

~ Hazrat Inayat Khan

Wounded Butterfly is my personal journey as a survivor from the dark side of love.

I am imprisoned by my past...

The ghosts will not leave.

Wounded Butterfly

I have walked in darkness. I have seen the edge of insanity. I have felt the depths of sorrow and despair. I have known the feelings of pain and suffering and the of loss of myself. The constant torment of my own mind.

But...

I also know what it feels like to see the light.

To feel happiness and strength.

To transform into someone, I am proud of.

To be able to quiet my mind and remind myself that I deserve better than what has happened to me.

To say to myself...

I AM NOT A VICTIM - I AM A SURVIVOR

Wounded Butterfly

_____

As I walked down the dark lonely road, I dared not look back.
So much had happened, and I only had so much strength to
take each step. Everything I owned was what I could carry in
my backpack and forty dollars in my pocket. The next part of
my journey had begun - my escape.

°• ✳ •°

The wind picks up the pieces of my broken heart and carries
them to a world unknown.

°• ✳ •°

It isn't where you come from that makes you who you are.
It's who you decide to be that makes you who you are.

Wounded Butterfly

I Remember

I remember the first time you yelled at me. I don't remember the words, but I remember the harshness of your voice.

I remember the first time you hit me. I don't remember why but I remember the pain and the fear I felt.

I remember every time after that and how I felt each time. Yes, I remember. Now all I am doing is trying to forget.

I went in search of love and found myself.

Wounded Butterfly

There are moments when everything is peaceful. Just as the sun is coming up, there's a tiny sliver of light coming through the opening of the curtains and I can hear the sounds of the day beginning. A blissful moment in time, all is well, and my heart is at ease. Then, a wave of despair washes over me, flooding my mind and heart as I remember - another day in Hell is about to begin, another day to survive, another day to stay alive.

°• ❋ •°

As I cover my battered and bruised body with my wounded wings, I listen to the raging storm that is you. The thunder of your voice howling in anger. The lightening of your hands as they hit the softness of my skin. Silently I whisper to myself, "please let the storm calm." Finally, there is quiet, the storm has passed; I have survived once again.

_____

With every breath I took loving you, I could slowly hear my heart breaking.

°• ✳ •°

As she picks herself up off the floor, ignoring the pain, she makes her way through the dark to the other room. She looks in the mirror, barely able to see, knowing it will look worse by morning. She wipes her face and a weak smile crosses her lips. She thinks to herself, "she has survived the hands of love again." For now, she is safe, and she will listen to his excuses and hollow apologies and he will be the man she loves, until the next time. Her shoulders slump as the first tear slides down her cheek and her knees hit the floor. Alone in the darkness she cries, as a little more of her heart dies.

Wounded Butterfly

The girl behind the door stood silent.

She would hide there quietly.

Listening to your footsteps as you walked.

Fearing your words, "We have to talk."

Barely taking a breath for fear you might hear the sound.

Silently praying not to be found.

She knew what it meant when you said those words.

They would be followed by her screams that nobody hears.

Yes, she knew it would be you that would win this round.

She would only be picking herself up off the ground.

It would be the last time, you will see.

Because the girl behind the door, yes that girl,

she used to be ME.

Wounded Butterfly

As I lay here all bruised and battered, the taste of my own blood sickening me again, the cruelty of his words still echoing in my head.

I wonder what I did this time to make him so angry. I hear a soft voice say, "All you did was love him."

As I slowly pull myself up through the pain and the tears, I walk away saying to myself, "Well, no more."

°• ✳ •°

You loved me to pieces, and I am still trying to put myself back together.

Wounded Butterfly

Him: His eyes have adjusted to the darkness. Slowly, methodically, he searches for his prey. Quietly, silently he listens for any sound. Suddenly a familiar scent, a sweet smell of blood; she's near. I will find her and this time she won't get away.

Her: In the darkness she lays hidden. Trying to slow her breathing. Trying not to make a sound. Blood dripping from her mouth, she wipes it away. Screaming inside her mind, please don't let him find me. Just this one time, let me get away.

Wounded Butterfly

Him: Holding her by her hair, knife at her throat, I say to her in a hushed tone, "I can smell your fear. You think you are so brave. Nobody cares about you. I can do anything I want. Who is going to help you now? I can push it just a little bit deeper and it would be all over."

Her: Looking at the evil in his eyes. Trying not to show fear. His breath reeks of alcohol and cigarettes. She says to him, "Go ahead, I don't care anymore." Waiting she steadies herself as he releases her. He looks at her with contempt in his eyes and slowly walks away, as he laughs. Another nightmare all too real, your hands were your knife and you used them well. How many times did we have this same standoff? How many times did you think you had won? I wonder, do you still feel you are the winner?

—————————

Him: Standing at the top of the stairs, he looks down at her. She will never believe it was an accident, he thinks to himself. Why doesn't she just listen to me? I told her to get rid of it. If she would only listen, I wouldn't have to hurt her so much. She just needs to learn to listen to me.

Her: Through half-closed eyes, she can see him standing at the top of the stairs. Trying to clear the fog in her mind. Trying to believe what he had done. Of course, it had to bean accident, he would never intentionally push her down the stairs. Slowly she replays what happened. He was holding her by the shoulders, screaming at her, "Get rid of it or I will, one way or another," he said. Then he let go. Oh my God, he called our baby an "it." "Get rid of it." Then he let go. As a sharp pain draws her back to the present time, she realizes what is happening. As the precious life inside her ebbs away, everything fades to black.

Wounded Butterfly

In Hell

I remember all the love we shared in the beginning. Happier times. The smiles and laughter; the light.

Then the darkness came. I don't remember what I did at that moment to bring it out of you. But I remember the look of hate in your eyes, the sting of your words.

This would be the beginning and the end.

So many times, you would say, "If you would only listen to me, then I would not have to hurt you."

It was then I realized when you lashed out at me with your words and you said to me, "Just go to hell."

I don't have to go, I'm already there.

Wounded Butterfly

When the memories of him hit me, I brace myself from falling. I feel as if the air has been sucked out of my lungs. I gasp for air, struggling to breathe but at the same time wanting it to be my last breath. I fight to live but I want to die. I know that living only allows my mind to torment my heart but to die would mean losing my soul. I can't let him win, I fought so hard to survive, to live. Yet at that moment, that awful blissful moment, there is peace in knowing the torment would end if I would just stop breathing.

°• ❋ •°

Here, take my heart. You have already ripped it apart anyway.

Wounded Butterfly

I wrapped my hands with bandages. I knew I could never fight you; I was not strong enough. So, I would fight the ghost of you until my hands were bloody. That is the only time I knew I could win.

°. ✳ .°

You always reminded me I belonged to you. Even when I refused you, you made sure I regretted saying no. You would have your way with me on your terms. Bloodied and bruised, I would hold myself together. Trying hard to keep my mind from breaking. It was not the first time and it would not be the last. I had a plan. Yes, I had a plan, I just had to stay strong enough to see it through.

Wounded Butterfly

You swore you would never lay another hand on me after the last time, but the truth is on my face. I stand here looking at you and I all I hear is your silence and the sound of my own heart beating.

°• ✳ •°

As I stood there looking at the mist covering the sea, a cold chill ran up my spine as memories flooded over me. So many times, I have stood here trying to forget - trying to remember. Was it always like this or did I just not see it, the monster you are?

°• ✳ •°

Your idea of love is a lonely road to hell.

Wounded Butterfly

It's funny how late at night I think of you. You will suddenly come to me in my dreams. I lay there wondering why at that same time most nights you come to me, then I remember. Even now so many years later I still fear the night and the sounds of silence. The silence is where I hear my screams the loudest, and they still ring in my ears.

°. ✳ .°

I still wake up from the nightmare of you. I can feel your hands still wrapped around my throat. Your voice ringing in my ears. Wake up, wake up -- I am not asleep.

Wounded Butterfly

It's three a.m. and I'm walking the floor again. Reliving the memories of you. Remembering how your hands felt on my skin. How your voice sounded in my ears. The pain of both on my body and my heart still lingers in my memory. It will be three a.m. tomorrow, see you then.

I am still chained in the dungeon of your evil. Laying in the filth of your words. Trying to escape from the torture of your memory. But how do I escape from my own mind?

Wounded Butterfly

Like the seasons you kept changing and not always for the better.

°• ❋ •°

He used his words as a weapon, cutting her so deeply, knowing the damage he was causing, but he didn't care. He knew she would never leave him; he had made sure of that. He would continue to attack her to the point of breaking her and then finally let up on her. He always knew how far he could push her. He could see it in her eyes. Those sad lifeless eyes of hers. Yes, she would never leave. He would always be her tormentor, and he enjoyed every minute of it.

I died again today. The memories came flooding over me. A wave of emotions I could not control. I felt as if I was standing at the edge of the ocean. The roar of the breakers coming to swallow me up. The deafening sound so beautiful but terrifying. I could not move, just watching as the water came closer. Waiting until the water would finally consume me. The end of my torment would finally be upon me. I would have the peace I craved so long for. Anxiously waiting for an end that would never come.

°• ✳ •°

Indifference -- the perfect weapon to kill love.

Wounded Butterfly

As I walk through the solitude of my darkness, the heaviness weighs upon my heart. The ghost of my memories no longer scares me. I am just waiting for the light to finally beckon me. I lay down upon the ground, weary of my journey but rest does not come easy. My soul bleeds for redemption that I fear will forsake me forever.

°● ✳ ●°

She walks the corridors of her heart, searching for answers she knows will never come. Gently she moves the silk drapes to peer into the darkness, watching. The crimson dress she wears reminds her of the blood she has so freely given up. The price of his love she knows has been too high. One day she will free herself from the guilt and finally forgive herself.

Wounded Butterfly

I went in search of love and found myself.

°. ✳ .°

She stands at the edge of eternity, looking beyond the place where the ocean meets the sky. In her loneliness, she feels safe as the solitude has become her friend. She can embrace her darkness; her memories are less haunting. In the quiet stillness of the night, she wanders, longing for the dawn not to come. The heaviness weighs upon her heart about roads not taken. How differently her life may have been. In her soul she knows, her destiny had already been written. Life had not always been good to her, but she still believes. She still believes.

Wounded Butterfly

———————

There is a quiet moment just as the sun dips below the
horizon when the day kisses the world goodnight. Twilight,
the time just before the darkness of night sets in. When all
the world is in the in-between time of day and night, the
gloaming. This was her time, her solitary moment of peace,
the brief moment of in-between. The time before the
darkness of her mind comes to haunt her.

°• ❋ •°

Her words had never meant anything to him. Her thoughts,
she kept tucked away in the recesses of her heart. Most of her
agony she kept deep inside. There are just some thoughts
that should never see the light of day.

Wounded Butterfly

Her heart was marred from the battlefield of love. The destruction had left wounds so deeply embedded she could not remember the last time she felt happy. She finally realized; love kills slowly. It didn't use a weapon. It used words and it used touch. That was the turmoil locked within her soul. She knew this was going to be the hardest battle to overcome.

°• ✳ •°

The biggest risk you will take, is to be seen for who you truly are.

Wounded Butterfly

As she looked upon her heart, she could feel it beating, struggling to live. She had ripped it out. The blood dripping warmly down her hands. It was not as she had expected. Suddenly a wave of unfamiliar emotions washed over her. She knew she was faced with a decision, live with the pain or die and escape. She could feel her strength diminishing. Death would give him pleasure, that thought she could not bear. Living meant she survived, and that would be the greatest victory of all.

°• ✳ •°

You can't wear makeup on your soul. It's either naturally beautiful or it's not.

Wounded Butterfly

I am with your ghost again. Quietly tiptoeing through the memories of you. Swaying back and forth between the good and the bad. Reflections blending together until they finally become one. Struggling to remember the beginning but trying to forget the ending. Stumbling around the darkness waiting for the light to save me.

°• ✳ •°

She killed her emotions and buried them deep in the ground. Some say they see her on moonless nights dancing amongst the gravestones. They can hear a soft melancholy hum whispering in the wind. She haunts all those who have seen her with beauty but they long to release her from her loneliness. Her story gets lost in the darkness as the sun breaks on the horizon.

Wounded Butterfly

There were times when I could feel your love. It felt like a whirlwind of emotions. Taking my heart to destinations I had never thought possible. It was so rare these special occasions that I would tuck them in my secret place. I would revisit them from time to time but as you became darker, it was harder to remember them. The darkness made your love selfish, controlling. You were not a man you were a devil. A wicked, vengeful devil who believed I was his to control and do to me as you wish, and it was my duty to comply. Compliance or else. The or else was always harsh and I would live in fear of them. Those moments still haunt me; those "or else" moments.

Wounded Butterfly

I have cried tears for you. I have felt the yearning for death in my darkest moments. The depths of my soul have felt primal fear. I no longer feel the essence of myself. My heart no longer beats for life, it beats only for survival. I am drowning in the pain of you and I do not have the strength to fight you anymore.

°. ✳ .°

Drowning in the memories of forgotten tears. You can hear her cries of agony within the depths of silence. Her sorrow filled wails haunt the night. Off in the distance, in the shadows, he listens. As her cries fade, he smiles.

Wounded Butterfly

When you knew I was falling, did you ever think about catching me? When my world was turning grey, did you ever think about bringing me a rainbow? When my tears started flowing, did you ever think about wiping them away? When my heart shattered, did you ever think about putting it back together? When I had lost all hope, did you ever think about giving me a reason not to let go? When my soul finally died, did you ever think about bringing me back to life?

Just once - did you ever, think about me?

°• ✳ •°

Part of me has given up but part of me still hopes.

Wounded Butterfly

How does one gauge another's pain? Does a single teardrop measure sadness? Is it within the eyes? Another's pain can never be truly measured unless you have seen inside of their soul. Touched the most inner sanctity of their most sacred place. The truest place of their soul the place they hold dearest. It is within this place that the purity of their feelings is most alive, where their true self lives, where the essence of their soul can be found. It is here, you can truly see, if you are really looking.

°● ✳ ●°

I always knew that darkness would be a part of me. Clinging itself to my innermost thoughts and emotions. Finding ways to extinguish the light within me.

Wounded Butterfly

If only you had walked away maybe I would still be me. If only you would have let me go, maybe I would still be free. If only you knew what love I was truly about, maybe would not be scarred. If only you knew what you had done, maybe I would not be still haunted. If only…

°• ✳ •°

I stay here lingering, surrounded by murky water. Waiting for the darkness to cover me. The cool air feels good against my warm battered skin. My body is growing tired, but I dare not move. I am so tired, so very tired but I must hold on. It is not safe for me to move until the darkness comes, then I can escape from him. But how will I escape the memories of him?

Wounded Butterfly

Our hearts are amazing, although broken and battered they still believe, still hope.

°• ✳ •°

Some say fight for the fairy tale - I don't believe in fairy tales anymore. I thought I was living mine. It turned out to be just a story; a fable you only wish you had read, not one you had lived.

°• ✳ •°

Once you learn the truth, don't let the devil through the front door again.

Wounded Butterfly

You once told me I did not have the strength to leave. I listened to your words and believed. The fear inside of me was so deep. Then there was the sound of silence. All I could hear was my heart pound. Now was my time to flee, to set myself free. Finally, I know what it feels like, to be you without me.

I have walked through Hell. I have looked the Devil in the eye. I have survived the fire of his fury. Not once did I back down or flinch from his touch. I would face him the rest of my days if I could, just to escape from the hell you put me through.

Wounded Butterfly

With a troubled and darkened soul, she walks in silence. She carries her torment in the labyrinths of her heart. She loses herself within the passages of memories. Trying to recollect the days before darkness came upon her, before her innocence was lost, before him. She continues her journey through the past as the melancholy consumes her. Leaving pieces of herself along the way.

She sits on the edge of eternity. The silence is so deafening she can barely hear the rhythm of her heart. She is drowning in past memories. Haunted by the ghost of you.

Wounded Butterfly

Always walk lightly on the hearts you touch.

°• ✳ •°

I have spent my life in purgatory. Trying to cleanse myself of the sins of you. The evil that you convinced me was mine, all along really belonged to you. The dark soulless demon that haunts me, I still cannot outrun. One day I will be released but you, you will spend eternity in the hell that you meant for me.

°• ✳ •°

From these chains I will rise.

Wounded Butterfly

I don't recognize myself anymore. The woman I was before you is no longer there. I search for her in my eyes, but she does not reflect back to me. You destroyed her long ago. Now I'm afraid I've lost her. I don't recognize myself anymore.

°• ❋ •°

In the moments of my solitude, I listen to the stillness, the silence of the quiet. I try to believe I will find my way out of the darkness. To believe in something. To still hope. To breathe even as the pain weighs so heavy upon my heart. Listening - just as I think I can no longer hold on; I hear my soul say to me, "I need you to be brave a little longer. I know you've lost your way, but I will be your light out of the darkness. Just believe, believe in you."

Wounded Butterfly

She felt so lost and alone; always searching, always hiding who she truly was, always afraid. Never sure who she could trust anymore with her heart. So, she locked it away from everyone. Taking the box that held it and burying it forever.

°● ❋ ●°

Dark is the hour. Quiet moments. Those long-gone moments that steal heartbeats from us now and then. Black polluted memories. Clutching our tarnished memories to our breast. Trying to pretend it was something else. Reliving the violence over in your mind. Blood runs. Listening to the voices in the silence. Your heart grows cold. The death of a soul.

Wounded Butterfly

She has felt the sharp edge of a razor against her skin. She has felt the burning ember of a cigarette against her lips. She has felt the drunken haze of alcohol the morning after. Yet none of them made her feel. All she wanted was just to feel, to feel alive, to be.

°• ❄ •°

Her eyes weep with tears unseen. The sound of silence echoes in her ears. Her heart screams with the agony of despair. Each new day is a reminder of the moment her soul died. Yet she still survives.

Wounded Butterfly

Sometimes the words we leave unsaid, actually free us.

°• ✳ •°

As I put another piece of me around my battered heart. Using my tears as glue to hold the makeshift wall together, I fall deeper and deeper into myself. I cannot outrun my darkest memories anymore. I don't have the strength to fight against the struggle. All I can do now is try to protect what is left of myself and my heart - hoping one day I will finally be able to set us both free.

°• ✳ •°

Some people thrive on chaos, don't be one of them.

Wounded Butterfly

I remember my deepest and darkest fears, late in the midnight hours. No-one really knows this pain inside of me. The crumbling of my heart as I try to hold myself together. How much my soul has endured. The chaos, the agony. I cannot find my safe haven. I am lost within the caverns of my own mind. I am my own warden, my own captive. I remain caged. I have no escape from the hell of myself.

°● ✳ ●°

In the chaotic sadness of my heart, I feel the emptiness grow heavier within my soul. It is a lonely feeling, like being a solitary passenger on a train to nowhere. Time passes unhurried and quickly at the same time.

Wounded Butterfly

You came into my dreams again. Taunting me with your love. Memories I try to forget in my waking hours. Wishing I could go back to the day we met. When you had not touched me yet. When I didn't know what your love was. When I still had control of my heart. When I knew what to do instead of being haunted by the ghost of you. You came into my dreams again and I woke up living in the nightmare you left me in.

°. ✳ .°

We all at one time of our lives wished for Death's hug.

I look inside myself and I see a black soul and a heart full of darkness.

°• ✳ •°

Between light and darkness, my black heart lingers. My soul dances in the shadows waiting for the suffering to end; to know how it feels not to be broken, beaten or bruised; to feel whole, to feel loved.

°• ✳ •°

May I know the value of myself above all else.

Wounded Butterfly

There is a heaviness in my soul I cannot understand. It feels as if I am in a deep sleep that I cannot awaken from. Oblivion is inevitable. Sadness has taken over. A vortex pulling me into a black hole. I will disappear soon. I will become nothing, and my soul will be lost. I will be a shell of myself, forever gone. I am no more.

°● ✳ ●°

The emptiness lies within my heart. I have locked my soul in solitude to protect the pieces that are left. My existence in the darkness has become my reality. One day I will stop wandering. My soul will finally find its way back into the light.

Wounded Butterfly

———————

Time holds no meaning for a soul that lives in darkness. Each moment feels like an eternity drowning in the depths of sadness. Your heart turns black without the light to embrace it. Once the roots of darkness take hold, you become part of the soulless. Lost in a dominion of shadows.

°• ✳ •°

You drag me through Hell and tell me it's Heaven.

°• ✳ •°

When your youthful innocence is stolen, a lake of numbing pain drowns your soul.

Wounded Butterfly

There is blood in the water. The wounds of my body have dripped many times within the same water. Even over time, the body learns to withdraw itself into a safe place. To not feel the pain at the moment but knowing the pain will be unbearable when the safe place is broken. But there is no safe place for the soul. It feels everything. The physical and emotional pain. The soul endures all things and when the soul can no longer carry the weight of the pain; There is blood in the water.

°∙ ✳ ∙°

I met evil as a child; nothing scares me now.

Wounded Butterfly

———————

When my past weighs heavily on my soul, and the pain in my heart will not let go, the memories flood over me and I hit the ground. The feelings of loss are so profound. Even the tears that come are all in vain and cannot wash away my pain. I long for the rain to come and cleanse me, to give me peace and set me free. Until I can find a way for the torment to end. The rain is my only friend.

°• ❋ •°

In my safe place, I can watch the world outside. Mostly, I can hide from the monster. He would never think to look for me here. Everyone thinks I'm afraid of the dark but I'm not. There are worse things to fear than the dark; it's where my little dreams get lost.

Wounded Butterfly

Dead, rotting, corpse reaching out for you even beyond the grave. Did you really think you could get away from what you had done? Did you think you could destroy her, and she would not haunt you? Did you think she would be forgotten? You will never forget; she will always be there to remind you. She will be your nightmare just as you were hers.

°• ✳ •°

I could smell the scent of stale cigarettes, and alcohol as you walked into the room. I didn't need the lights on to know where you had been. I, like so many nights before, tried so desperately to pretend I was sleeping. When I was lucky, it worked but on those nights it didn't... please let it be one of those nights.

Wounded Butterfly

People will always run from the truth but will stay for a lie.

°• ✳ •°

She heard his voice even in the quietness of the sky. Even the loudness of her heartbeat could not drown out his voice in her head. The worst kind of sadness would come over her. Even his cruelty she missed because now all she felt was lost and lonely. Even the worst of him was better than not having him.

Now, who is really the cruel one?

🦋

Wounded Butterfly

No matter how many times I have tried, the water just won't cleanse the touch of you. Trust broken, innocence stolen, our secret. Just a child, you killed her, but she lives. Now, all that's left is a hollow shell, with unbearable pain that has shattered her soul.

There is a satisfying thought I hold within my heart. After surviving you and the horror you felt I deserved. Death has a mark by my name. But don't worry, I will be waiting for you. I will be the one who finally gets to say, "Go to Hell, you worthless piece of shit."

Wounded Butterfly

I sit here alone in my darkness. My memories begin to
overtake me. They take me back to the beginning, the loss of
my innocence. I was always raised to believe you were safe
with family. But it's not true, family can be monsters. They
creep into your nightmares and tell you, "It's a special game."
Who would believe a 5-year-old, anyway? You learn how to
avoid them but when you can't, all you can do is scream in
your head. Finally, he leaves you alone but there's someone
else lurking about, waiting. So many years of pretending I
was just a toy, meant to be played with. Surviving the
memories by pretending. But sadly, this is all you know, and
you have carried these memories with you and the scars have
festered quietly below the surface. And each time the love
you receive takes you back; pretending I am a toy again.

Wounded Butterfly

I Am... and that is enough.

In the forest of my mind, I saw the ghost of the girl I used to be. I was afraid to approach her. How could I tell her how sorry I am for letting her down? How could I let her see what we have become?

I am not afraid of the shadows that follow me in the darkness anymore. They are remnants of my past demons that still try to haunt me.

The Little Girl

As I stood in the shadows. I watched the little girl. Quietly she sat there. I wonder if she would listen if I tried to talk to her. Try to reassure her that life doesn't always stay in this moment. That there will be times of happiness. That not everyone she meets will be a monster. That she, even if she doesn't believe it now, will survive what life throws her way. But I know it's too late, the seeds of darkness have already been planted in her soul. The sadness of her heart was already in her eyes. Sadly, her innocence had already been stolen, she was already lost. She would be one of those lonely souls forever searching for her way home, a journey she had to walk alone.

As I continue to watch her, wiping the tears from my cheeks, it is then I realized, the little girl was me and I was reliving a memory.

Wounded Butterfly

Most of us believe the devil has a face, but those of us who truly know, the devil is sometimes sitting right next to you.

When I think of you, it feels as if the water is pouring down around me. Slowly trying to cover me until I disappear. Lost beneath the surface, I am no longer myself. Finally, the pain of yesterday is gone, and the darkness has been drowned.

Wounded Butterfly

She was still a little girl in a woman's body. Frightened of everything and everybody. As she stood in the corner watching all the monsters, she wondered what they looked like behind their masks. The fear was becoming stronger as she tried to disappear into the wall. She trusted no-one except Dolly and now they were both trapped.

"Dolly, I'm scared, what should we do? Should we stay and wait for the monsters to leave or run and hide?"

"Run," said Dolly.

So, we ran and ran and ran and, we never looked back.

Wounded Butterfly

This face never scared me. It was the face you showed the world that scared me the most.

°• ❋ •°

I was falling to the ground as you were standing above me, my hands outstretched because my wings were dying, but you let me fall, you didn't care as my heart shattered and my soul scattered. You just turned around and walked away. The echoes of your laughter still ringing in my ears.

°• ❋ •°

I have seen evil but the evil that terrified me the most was the look in your eyes just before the storm.

Wounded Butterfly

There was a time when your words of hate would have crushed me. They would have left me bruised and broken. My heart bleeding and shattered. My soul ripped apart.

Not anymore, you no longer have that power. I have picked myself up and moved forward away from your darkness. I slayed the demons you tried to plant inside of my mind, heart, and soul.

I am free.
I am free.

Wounded Butterfly

Reflections of Me

As I sit here with my memories and wonder how I survived. The love I thought would be mine forever was lost. In what seemed to be in an instant, you changed into someone I did not recognize. And yet, all I can see are the "*Reflections of Me*" you said made you change.

The hands that once caressed me soon created pain. The voice that was soothing with the sound of love, would scream with hate. The eyes that held the look of love, were filled with contempt. The heart that was once mine, would beat for another.

The changes you say I caused, you made sure you reminded me of them every day. Me, the unworthy, the one who doesn't deserve you. Yes, I see the "*Reflections of Me*" through your eyes but one day you will see the "*Reflections of You*" in mine, and then you will see who was the unworthy one.

Wounded Butterfly

When silence screams, you can hear your heartbreaking the moment the soul dies.

°• ❋ •°

Death dances lightly in everyone's shadow. Slowly within the rhythm of your life. A silent partner waiting to take the lead. A graceful interlude.

°• ❋ •°

I have lived a lifetime in a single moment and have died in the same moment. That moment meant the most. Because when I died, I was able to escape from you. If only for a moment.

Wounded Butterfly

Death cannot harm me. I have lived in his shadow most of my life. I have seen the way he torments a soul into believing you should fear him. No, Death cannot harm me because you are not Death. You are just a man too weak to be anything else.

°• ✻ •°

It's too late, the rose has died. The smell of death and decay lingers in the air. The web of deceit has already been spun. Terror has reached out and it needs to be fed. Nothing is as it seems.

Wounded Butterfly

She walks a line between life and death. Life and its promises of hope. Death and its promises of release.

°•�֎•°

Death hovered over her. Patiently waiting for the malady to overtake her. She laid there in her glorious beauty. Her wings ready but her heart still unsure. He had tried to take her before. Was she strong enough to overcome his desire for her again? In her moment of uncertainty, she knew she must be. For now, she will remain in stasis, growing stronger, waiting for the perfect moment to emerge. The moment he would be at his weakest. That will be her moment, her perfect moment.

Wounded Butterfly

I felt death would consume me, but I could not let him win. I could hear the chants of evil surrounding me. They were luring me to them. He was still above me watching, hoping to see the end but I would live just to spite them all.

°• ✳ •°

Our lives are but a series of moments. Memories that someone else will remember for us. For it is in one's death when the true purpose and meaning of their life reveals what it was truly about.

°• ✳ •°

I no longer let you hold your death sentence over me. Taunting my heart, tearing pieces of my soul apart.

Wounded Butterfly

In a world full of noise, all I hear is the silence of my own emptiness.

°• ✻ •°

As I walk through the corridors of my mind and if the wind is blowing them, the curtains that are my memories, move with each passing moment. In the darkest recesses of my soul, the echoes of my past haunt me. I am slowly trying to find my way back into the light, but the demons continue to tug at me. Slowly I move, hoping beyond hope that one day I will make it back.

°• ✻ •°

You never did understand. Death was never the end game, survival was.

Wounded Butterfly

Did you really think I was to be conquered? A pliable but savage land to discover, a soft but wild creature to tame? It didn't matter to you if I was willing; I was your prey. It was a game of power, and you were in it to win no matter the cost. If it meant a total annihilation of my soul, then you would make sure of it. You underestimated me. You did not expect me to be a worthy adversary. Me, the weak creature, the lesser of us, but I rose above you. I fought, and you could not control me. In the end, it was I who would escape. It was me who held the power. And you, you would never win, and I would never be tamed.

°. ✳ .°

She is forgiving even when she is aching.

Wounded Butterfly

My heart is a graveyard full of memories longing to finally rest in peace.

°• ❋ •°

Some memories just won't let you go. Time passes slowly and years may pass but yet they linger as if it was just a moment ago. The pain flows through your body, and for a moment you are back in the horror. Slowly you pull yourself out of the memories, gasping for breath, trembling as you hold your tears at bay.

°• ❋ •°

I hope when my life ends and my heart fades to black; you remember who I was and not what I had become.

Wounded Butterfly

—————————

I am a solitary soul. Fear has become my shadow.
Like a single flower standing alone, afraid of being crushed.

Alas, my soul like the flower, the beauty of which will never
be known.

°• ✳ •°

Pain has a way of reminding us there is a part of us still alive.
Some types of pain, however, run so deep it is a constant
reminder we wish to forget. Especially if it is a pain inflicted
by someone we love. We must remember, we did nothing to
deserve the pain we feel and somehow, we must find a way
to forgive ourselves.

Wounded Butterfly

Broken Angel

Why can't I silence the chaos? Why indeed the voices in her head asked.

They weren't voices, she knew; they were her Demons.

Only in the darkness did they come, begging her to come out and play.

She pleaded with them for silence if only for a moment.

Still, they chanted, "*Broken Angel come over to the darkness, we want to play.*"

Still, she screamed for silence, screams only she could hear.

"*Broken Angel come over to the darkness, we want to play.*", the Demons continued.

Only in the darkness did she let herself feel broken.

Only in the darkness did she feel strong enough to fight her Demons.

"*Broken Angel come over to the darkness, we want to play.*"

"*I am not a Broken Angel,*" she screamed. "*I am a Wounded Angel.*"

Finally, the Demons fell silent, at least for a moment.

A silent blissful moment.

_____

Tears of an Angel

The sadness must be deep to make an Angel cry.

Falling to the ground after flying so high.

Broken and battered she must truly be.

Pain that has been hidden but now can be seen.

Tears of an Angel rolling down her cheeks.

Words not spoken but yet her heart still speaks.

°• ✳ •°

I am a creature of the night. I roam in the darkness, the moonlight as my guide. The sounds of the night are the music of my heart. My soul is at home here in the beauty of the night.

Wounded Butterfly

Darkness is overwhelming my heart, and my soul feels heavy.

°• ✳ •°

Sometimes the heart sees what is invisible to the eye. Does it mean we ignore what we feel or what we see? In life we let our emotions rule our lives more than we should at times. We see with our hearts and ignore what our soul is telling us. We want to see the good in all things because that is what our heart wants. But sometimes, what is invisible to the heart is visible to the soul. Those are the moments we must really see.

Wounded Butterfly

When the first rays of sunshine come across the horizon, it is a beautiful sight.

I look at it through the trees and wonder what it would be like to walk into the light.

For a moment I reach out and let the light touch my fingertips. The warmth is surprising to me.

Then I hear them calling me, the demons I hide from in the dark and I turn around and flee.

°• ✳ •°

The wind picks up the pieces of my broken heart and carries them to a world unknown.

Wounded Butterfly

Cries in the Night

There are cries in the night that go unheard. Silent whimpers of heartbreak and sorrow, we can no longer contain.

Cries that are hidden when the sky cries with rain. Letting us know it also feels our pain.

Silently we tremble as we gather our thoughts. Until the next time, the cries in the night come. No-one will know the battle we fought.

I sit in the shadows, afraid. I am trying to silence my mind. Trying to shut out the ugliness of my past demons.

I see the light and spread my wings. Take flight, I think, and I will be free. If only, yes if only...

Wounded Butterfly

I need to heal my soul and silence my mind so I can find peace. I need to find my inner strength and courage to find my way out of the darkness.

°• ❋ •°

If you wait until you are ready, you will be waiting for the rest of your life. Trust your soul and spread your wings. Even if you feel your wings are not ready, you can always learn how to fly as you fall.

°• ❋ •°

In the stillness of the night, I listen. I can hear the wounded souls' cries of agony. They beg for the release of all the heartbreak that is tormenting them.

Wounded Butterfly

What is keeping them here in the darkness? Why don't they fly out of the darkness into the light? Are they like me, forever trapped?

We are all the lost and wounded souls of the night.

°• ✳ •°

Your meaning of 'until death do us part' is, "If you ever try to leave me, I will kill you."

Betrayal

What is betrayal in a relationship? Is it physical infidelity, emotional infidelity, mental thought or a moment of weakness? Is it betrayal if the other person doesn't know of the betrayal?

Betrayal is betrayal no matter what type it is. Just because the other person doesn't know about the betrayal doesn't make it less of a betrayal. A sin is still a sin. A lie is still a lie.

Sometimes the person may know of the betrayal but chooses not to acknowledge it because then the betrayal becomes real. But inside their heart is breaking and a crack has formed that may never be able to be repaired.

If you think you have not betrayed the person that loves, you because they may not know of your betrayal; you may want to think again. That is the biggest betrayal of all.

Wounded Butterfly

─────────

I may be able to forgive you for a physical betrayal. But an emotional betrayal cuts deep into my soul and it is a scar that never heals.

My trust for you becomes like a broken mirror. You can try to repair it, but no matter what, I'll always see the cracks.

The truth is none of us are immune from betrayal. We give our trust in hopes of it not being betrayed. Sometimes even if it is unintentional it happens. What we must decide is how we handle the betrayal. Trust is often the hardest to rebuild. So, use it wisely.

Wounded Butterfly

The Mirror

I look in the mirror, and what do I see.

I do not recognize the woman looking back at me.

I see an aged tormented soul, eyes filled with tears.

Telling the stories of pain, she has endured throughout the

years.

Sadness she has lived, the words she has heard.

Love that was said but has never been hers.

I look in the mirror and what do I see.

I see the woman he has made out of me.

Looking in the mirror to see what would be looking back at

me, I realized it wasn't a demon; it was the devil, and he was

laughing for me to see.

Wounded Butterfly

Nothing is more heartbreaking than the sadness of the soul.

°. ❋ .°

It is hard to believe the things you say to me, even if your words are true. You lose faith in the one you love from all the things they do. When all that is left is heartbreak, you harden the shell around you; always fearing you may breakthrough. I don't know if I can trust you, what is a heart to do?

Wounded Butterfly

I used to remember the things you would say to me. The sweet nothings I would so fondly call them. Your eyes never betrayed the deception behind your words. The lies you told flowed so smoothly from your lips. You were really good at the game, but in the end, I began to see the words you so freely spoke were never meant for me.

°. ✳ .°

If we can keep love in our hearts, then we all have one more day we can say we survived the darkness.

Wounded Butterfly

Try

Trying to heal a heart that has gone cold as ice and been closed for so long.

Trying to remove the stains of red from the guilt of past sins that are not even mine.

Trying to wake up my soul that has become black as pitch.

Trying to learn how to fly again.

°• ✳ •°

In the darkness, with each heartbreak, I want to give up. I try so hard not to lose faith. It is then I can hear my soul whispering, softly encouraging me - "*Don't give up, even a Wounded Butterfly can fly.*"

Wounded Butterfly

I hung up my wings because you convinced me I was unworthy of flying. Now I'm trying to convince myself that you were wrong.

°• ✲ •°

Killing me softly they land upon my hand. Their wings feel like velvet as I steady myself. Black as midnight but their beauty astounds me.

°• ✲ •°

Sometimes, inside my head is a very dark place. The longing for peace is unattainable. The demons are dancing around with so much joy while causing me so much sorrow.

Wounded Butterfly

I feel numb inside. Sometimes it's so expansive that it bleeds into the shadows I have surrounded myself in. Filling the black void around me. Allowing the aching emptiness to spill inside and settle, blanketing my heart.

°• ✳ •°

There were so many times I wished I was invisible. So many times, I wanted to melt away from your gaze. So many times, just to be unseen.

°• ✳ •°

The past doesn't always stay buried. It finds its way back, clawing and digging until it finds you. Reaching for you with its bloody hands.

Wounded Butterfly

I go through the motions of life sorting through the memories of my past. I try to file them away and destroy the ones I wish to forget. Cleaning out the files that I no longer need. Reorganizing my mind. Funny how I try to convince myself that I can do this. Bury them in file thirteen - things to be destroyed. If only it was that easy.

To be brave is to love someone unconditionally, without expecting anything in return. It takes courage to just give because we don't want to fall on our faces or leave ourselves open to hurt.

Darkness

Darkness comes to me, covers me like a blanket. Holds me close to its bosom, so tightly I feel as if I cannot breathe.

Darkness comes to me, whispers softly in my ear, "I am you and you are me." "Why are you still fighting it, why don't you see?"

Darkness comes to me, I finally let go. How can I continue to fight with such a worthy foe?

Darkness comes to me, I cannot hide. I wait for the daylight hoping for relief, only to realize, Darkness follows me wherever I go.

Wounded Butterfly

The truest measure of friendship is not in the words that are spoken or by the actions done. It can only be truly measured by how the heart feels and by the love that touches the soul.

Pull me out of this darkness in which I dwell.
Show me the light of love in your heart.

We each walk in our own darkness. It is not for us to judge another. Those of us that may suffer in silence, may be looking for someone to show us the way back into the light.

Wounded Butterfly

Sometimes in life, the best friendships are the ones that are unexpected; that develop when they are most needed. For it is those that remind us in our darkest moments, anything is possible if we just believe. A friendship that needs no words to be explained but is felt in the heart and touches your soul. These friendships are to be cherished and held close - always.

°∙ ✳ ∙°

Sometimes late at night when I am all alone, lying in bed in the darkness, the demons dancing inside of my head; I pray that someone will come and save my soul. Who will come and fight for me, when I cannot even fight for myself?

Wounded Butterfly

No matter how much you revisit the past, there's nothing new to see! That's why it's called the past. Keep moving forward.

°• ✳ •°

Each of us walks our own path through life. It is not for others to judge the decisions we make during our journey. There are no right or wrong turns, that is for destiny to decide. If we continue to let the opinions of others create our decisions for us, then we destroy our own destiny. So never let anyone tell you they know what is best for you. Only you are walking your path.

Wounded Butterfly

Behind my eyes... Emptiness

Tears wept in silence

A story of a wounded butterfly

A heart that died yet still beats

A soul that has been lost in darkness

Behind my eyes... Hope

°• ✳ •°

Release the bounds of your demons, set them free. They can only hold you if you let them. They are the darkness within, but you are the light. They grow stronger the harder you fight. Let them go, let them go.

Wounded Butterfly

Tears

There are different kinds of tears we cry. Some tears can help us while others can hurt us. Tears of joy or tears of sadness. Tears that make us feel like we cannot escape our darkness. Tears that free us from our bonds. The worst kind of tears are the tears we don't cry. The tears that we have held for so long inside of us we are afraid to let them go. These are the tears that we must release. The tears that we must let flow. The tears we don't ever show.

°• ❋ •°

I walk my path with strength and with purpose. I walk with renewed hope that today my path will lead me to my destiny. As long as I keep walking my path, it will lead me where I am meant to be.

Wounded Butterfly

_____

Today

Today I'm not going to let my pain destroy me.

Today I'm not going to let the thoughts of others about me
matter.

Today I'm not going to let my darkness consume me.

Today I'm not going to let the words of others hurt me.

Today I'm not, because today I am.

°• ✳ •°

Sometimes we go through life lost, not sure what direction
we want to travel. We suffer pain and loss and we feel our
lives are wasted. We finally get to a point we must decide,
"What is our purpose?"

If you want to find your purpose in life, find your wound.

Wounded Butterfly

_____

I am sitting here alone with my thoughts. I feel as if I have lost my way somewhere in the darkness. I am trying to get my heart back. I feel as if my soul is bleeding.

°. ✳ .°

Even the tears that come are all in vain and cannot wash away my pain. I long for the rain to come and cleanse me, to give me peace and set me free; until I can find a way for the torment to end. The rain is my only friend.

°. ✳ .°

Memories are haunted places we visit from time to time.

Wounded Butterfly

Sometimes in the quiet moments, I hear the sound of my inner voice whispering to me, "*You are worthy of everything beautiful.*"

I try to remember that when the darkness of my mind taunts me, but there are moments when it becomes difficult.

And yet, here I am... still listening.

°• ✳ •°

Once we learn to pray with our hearts, and not our lips we truly begin to have a conversation with God. It is in the midst of the silence you can hear God speaking the loudest.

Wounded Butterfly

The demons that live inside of my tortured mind are haunting me again. One by one I can hear them chanting. "You are worthless, everybody will betray you, nobody loves you." Then in unison their final horrifying chant, "We are all you have."

I try to run from the sound of their deafening voices. Only to realize that I cannot run away from them. They live inside my mind. They will forever taunt me until I can find my way back into the light.

°• ✳ •°

I'm not afraid to be alone. Some of my most peaceful moments have been in the midst of solitude.

Wounded Butterfly

In the dark night of my soul, I linger. As the memories flood over me, I slide deeper into the bowels of darkness. I continue to travel from the light to the dark.

°• ✳ •°

I have been down this road before. Taking one step at a time. Each step moving one more step forward towards the light. I can hear the hounds of hell screaming, they are my demons. It feels as if they are nipping at my heels trying to drag me back into the pit of despair. But I must keep fighting, I must. I cannot let the darkness consume me. I must not let my demons win; I must not let them win... Not again.

Wounded Butterfly

When I gave you my heart, I didn't know you would give it back to me all bloody and torn apart with wounds so deep it would never heal.

°. ✻ .°

Butterflies, butterflies fly away free,

Take all of my dreams with you for all the world to see.

Fly high and fly low and all through the night.

Spread your wings in Heavenly flight.

When you are done and you are ready to come home,

Remember always you were never alone.

Wounded Butterfly

If you could write a story about your heart, what would it say? Would the chapters be filled with the scars of your soul? Each line describing the sadness and heartbreak it has endured. Would there be chapters filled with happiness?

Each of us are in control of our own story, make it a great one.

°• ✳ •°

Save me from the nothingness that I've become. Instead of the pain and sorrow of this hell.

Wounded Butterfly

In relationships there are mistakes made, feelings are hurt, and words are said in anger. Once you try to correct the mistake, even when you feel you are not wrong, you are doing it because you want to salvage what may be left; if anything. You try to recover, begin to heal, and move forward. If, however, the other person cannot meet you halfway, accept it when you reach out, and continues to hold the hurt and anger in their heart, what are you to do?

Sometimes all you can do is move on and call it a day. Sometimes no matter what you do, it will never be enough.

°. ❋ .°

She had the mind of a serial killer. Trying to murder every memory of you until there was nothing left but an empty shell.

Wounded Butterfly

There is dark within and without, and it will sow the seeds of doubt. But there is also light within us, that we must never let go out. We must be our own champion, and we must always be the victor in our story.

°• ✳ •°

Memories of yesterday continue to haunt me. No matter what I do, they will not set me free. They are with me night and day. In my mind, they taunt me as if they are a movie stuck on replay. Even daylight is no longer my friend. I just keep waiting for the darkness to end.

Wounded Butterfly

———————

Sometimes in love and in life, we stumble. Things don't always go as planned. We can choose to value the lessons we take away from the experience or we can choose to let it harden our heart. Taking the pain and letting it turn into bitterness and destructive behavior only creates more turmoil for us. If we can keep the hate from blinding us from the lessons, then however painful the experience, we can be grateful and move forward.

°. ❊ .°

When his hands reached to help me, I flinched. There were too many uncounted times that his hands were searching for more than just helping.

My Nightmare

Darkness consumes me and covers me like a blanket. Fills me
with dread and despair. Flooding my memories and drowns
me with sorrow. I cannot wake from the nightmare that
torments me. The demon I thought I once slayed has come
back even stronger and will not let go. The chain that binds
me is still in the demon's hand, taunting me. Even my silence
will not drive it away. It screams to be heard, it screams for
me to answer but I must not, I cannot, I will not.

°. ✳ .°

I did not choose to live in the shadows surrounded by
darkness. It was within the light that darkness found me.
Now it will not let me go.

I have lost my soul to the darkness, and death feels like a beautiful escape.

°• ❋ •°

Unconditional Love

The heart wants what it wants. The heart feels what it feels. Your heart does not understand loving any other way but unconditionally, unless you teach it to. If you love someone, you love them flaws and all; good and bad. Even things you may not understand or agree with. This does not mean you let your heart be broken or stepped on by those who cannot love you unconditionally in return. You protect yourself but you don't change who you are. Because in the end, that is what love is truly about.

Wounded Butterfly

When you close your eyes, no-one can see. They cannot see your broken heart. They do not know you are trying to hide the sadness in your eyes. They don't know the years of struggle you are hiding, the years of pain or the longing for peace, a moment of silence from the demons that still haunt you. They cannot see your broken soul. When you close your eyes, no-one can see.

°● ✳ ●°

As the mist surrounded her, she accepted her darkness and let it carry her home.

Wounded Butterfly

_____

You stand back in the shadows pushing me down. You think you cannot be seen trying to take my wings. But look closely and see, you are the demon standing above me.

°• ✳ •°

There was a time I believed you when you said, "I'm high on loving you." The moments you would make me feel like I was your angel; I was your heaven on earth.

Then you became my hell on earth. The love you so freely gave me you started holding from me. It started coming with a price, a price too high for me to pay.

Wounded Butterfly

———————

Tears are a way for our heart to speak when we cannot find the words to explain our pain. Silence speaks when our soul is broken.

°. ✳ .°

I lost myself in your darkness. I thought it was your way of loving me. I did not realize you were ravishing my soul for your own amusement. You had a way of making the pain seem beautiful almost intoxicating. But it was poison, a slow death that I needed to escape. I lost myself in your darkness. Now I am just trying to find my way back into my light.

Wounded Butterfly

I remember falling and in the midst of darkness, I could see the monster's face staring down at me. Watching me as I fell deeper in the bowels of hell.

°•✳•°

Healing doesn't come quickly enough when the heart is broken, and the soul is tired.

Wounded Butterfly

———————

When my past starts to weigh heavy on my soul,
  and the pain in my heart will not let go.
The memories flood over me, and I hit the ground.
The feelings of loss are so profound.

°• ✳ •°

I have stood in the rain for so long,
  but no amount of water can wash away my pain.
I longed for peace to come over me.
Heal my heart and let me be.
Still, I cry and hurt even more.
I just beg let it rain, let it pour,
  I don't want to hurt anymore.

Wounded Butterfly

As I stand here trying to decide

Stay with what is behind me

 or cross to the other side

Not sure because I cannot see,

 but I know I want to be free

From a past filled with pain

 to a future with much to gain

Cross the bridge to the unknown

 and let my heart surely see

What it's like to finally be

Sadness

Why is it so hard for people to understand, that sadness is not a way of life? It isn't a cry for attention. Unlike a physical wound, it heals, maybe not completely, but it heals to a scar you can slightly see. An emotional scar even if you can't see it, is still a wound. Sometimes it is so deep, nothing can help ease the pain or the sadness. It just takes time. When you want to be alone, it isn't because you are being antisocial. Sometimes, the only person who understands your sadness is you.

Wounded Butterfly

I always thought everyone who said they loved me, meant it. Sadly, most people love you because of the way you love them.

°• ✳ •°

We all have memories we keep buried in the midnight gardens of our minds.

°• ✳ •°

There is a haunting pain that covers your heart. The overwhelming silence of an ending, when time stops.

Wounded Butterfly

Ghost of Myself

"Can you hear me?" I'm screaming, but nobody can.
"Can you see me?" I'm screaming, but nobody can.

They stopped listening to me so long ago.
They stopped seeing me even longer before that.

There is beauty in this, I think to myself.
Beauty, yes, because I am just a ghost of myself.

Wounded Butterfly

Shattered

Shattered pieces of my heart,
  you came and tore my world apart.
Without a word you left and walked away.
Even as I begged for you to stay.
Now after all these years I finally see.
It was always about you, never about me.

°• ✳ •°

Let the ocean take me. Let me feel the waves carry me
beyond the horizon past the sunrise. Let the wind erase the
memories of days of long ago and fill my heart with the midst
of tomorrow. Let my soul feel free as the sea, as I finally
come back to me.

Wounded Butterfly

Some memories just won't let you go. Time passes slowly, and years may pass and yet they linger; as if it was just a moment ago. The pain flows through your body and for a moment you are back in the horror. Slowly you pull yourself out of the memories. Gasping for breath, trembling you hold your tears at bay.

°• ✳ •°

I would rather walk through a dark day in Hell alone than to be accepted by the crowd trying to steal their way into Heaven.

°• ✳ •°

The real tragedy in life is everyone will love you until they see you as competition.

Wounded Butterfly

Forgotten Places

She hides in the forgotten places, broken and battered by heartbreak. She feels safer there because she can be alone and stay lost. The forgotten places nobody wants to see, a place where she can just be.

°• ✳ •°

Heartbeats

You once told me you could not imagine one beat of your heart without me. Then the day came I finally realized, I was only worthy of one beat of your heart, but you were every beat of mine.

Wounded Butterfly

———————

Sadly, I must distance myself to save myself from people. Some people just don't have good intentions. I get tired; I admit it, people drain me. Just be kind, it's not that difficult.

°• ✳ •°

My heart has turned cold. My soul has turned black. Even my darkness cannot comfort me.

Wounded Butterfly

Faces

I tried to show my true face so you could look into my eyes. I wanted you to see into my heart and deep within my soul. All the secrets I have carried but was afraid to show. I thought I had finally found another I could trust. Someone who could love me back to the light. But you only saw a way to hurt me. You used my secrets to drive me deeper into the darkness. Now I wonder if it's the faces of me that will ever be seen. Or if I will be left here as it has been meant to be.

Wounded Butterfly

I'm not afraid of the darkness anymore, it's the daylight that scares me the most. That's when the real monsters come out.

°• ❋ •°

There is a story behind my eyes I hold deep within my soul and battered heart. A journey from the darkness back into the light. The strengthening of my wings so I can finally take flight.

°• ❋ •°

Sometimes in the middle of all the chaos, you find your true self.

Wounded Butterfly

The Beauty of the Butterfly

Alone in the darkness, a caterpillar wraps itself in the safety of a cocoon, protecting its fragile body from harm. Slowly it begins a transformation, a journey to become what it is meant to be. Once it is ready with the transformation complete, it emerges into the light. A beautiful butterfly for all the world to see. Although it may be just for a short amount of time, its beauty is a sight to behold. Its beauty remembered.

Wounded Butterfly

_____

So many nights I lay down screaming. Pleading for help. Please, just hear me but help never comes because the screaming is only in my head.

There are so many ways a heart can break. Suffering a loss that wounds you to the core of your soul. Like living with the memory of holding your baby as her heart takes its last beat and knowing, "This is what it feels like to die."

Wounded Butterfly

My smile is my mask. It hides the loneliness that fills my
heart and the sadness that touches my soul. But there are
times I feel the lonely tears fall down my face and the mask
slips away.

°• ❋ •°

Memories have flooded over me, drowning me in their
darkness. Covering the light in my heart, shadowing my soul.
Happiness continues to elude me; sadness fills me with
emptiness. My eyes have no tears, they cry without weeping.
My voice no longer sings, it only speaks in silence.

Wounded Butterfly

Each scar I have describes the sadness and heartbreak my heart has endured. Little reminders of a life filled with torment and pain. Although you may not see my scars, they are there between each beat of my heart. And yet, here I am.

°• ❀ •°

I think we feel the heartache most at night. At the end of the day, our hearts just want to be home. But our homes aren't always where we rest our heads.

Wounded Butterfly

Anatomy of a Broken Heart

There are moments when it seems time moves in slow
motion. When life and time conspire together to make sure
you remember every detail of the memory that is about to be
created. Then it happens, that sorrow filled sound from your
throat. The crack of your voice when you are on the verge of
crying. The feeling as if all the air has been pulled out of your
lungs. The unsteadiness you feel but you are sitting down.
Then you realize, it is at that very moment, you can actually
feel your heartbreak. What has taken but a moment in time
feels like an eternity and nothing after that moment feels the
same ever again.

Wounded Butterfly

She chases butterflies in the darkness just to feel alive. She lets the moon guide her along the way. She clings to a single white rose as a reminder of that fateful day, when her heart broke and her soul slipped away.

°• ❋ •°

If pain had a face, would you look at the world with more understanding or with more indifference?

Wounded Butterfly

Soul Sick

I step into the light and I feel the sun burn my skin. I long to go back into the darkness but I force myself to stay.

There is beauty in the light if I can just see it. More beauty than what I see in the darkness.

If only he was here with me, maybe I could. My heart mourns for his touch, his lips on mine. He is the light, but I am the darkness. My heart cries, my soul is sick.

I look again into the light at the beauty of it all. I then return to the darkness forever alone.

Wounded Butterfly

You can let the darkness destroy you or you can bloom, but remember, you can't lie to your soul.

I used to believe one of the worst feelings I could imagine was being an outsider in a world full of insiders, but I was wrong, knowing I am is worse.

We all live in a state of in-between - between whom we were and who we want to be.

Wounded Butterfly

_____

Days

There are some days I don't want to feel OK.

Days I want to just feel the pain.

Days I want to cry tears like falling rain.

Days that turn into nights and back into day.

Days that I feel so completely drained.

These are the days I just don't want to feel OK.

Wounded Butterfly

Darkness can be all-consuming; it can suck the life out of you. It asks for your undivided attention and doesn't let you go. It doesn't care who you are or what you do, it will, if you let it, take over everything.

°• ✳ •°

Isn't it sad that we wake up every day alive, yet we are dead inside?

Wounded Butterfly

Can you hear it? The breaking of my heart.

Can you hear it? The howls of agony my soul cries in the quiet.

Can you hear it? The drops of my tears as they hit the ground.

Can you hear it? The loudness of no sound.

°• ✳ •°

Sometimes, we are just looking for that one star in our dark sky to help us find our way back home to ourselves.

Wounded Butterfly

We all have the capacity to forgive but who forgives us when we cannot forgive ourselves.

°• ❋ •°

My forgiveness is not offered to those who deserve it or don't deserve it. My forgiveness is offered to have peace in my heart. I do not hold bitterness towards those who have betrayed me or hurt me. I forgive them because I have moved on and I am no longer a prisoner to the pain. I may have forgiven you, but I will never forget.

Wounded Butterfly

Sometimes slamming the door before you say goodbye is the best way to leave.

°• ✳ •°

No one ever knows that silence has a voice and when it speaks it tells almost everything.

°• ✳ •°

We are all guilty of letting our past hold us hostage. It's time to pay the ransom and set ourselves free.

Wounded Butterfly

Sometimes your soul whispers to you in quiet moments. It speaks to you when you are looking for the answers you are seeking. When you no longer trust your heart, it will guide you. It is then you really need to listen, it will show you the way.

°• ✳ •°

She walks across the ruins of hell. Each step she takes is another demon she leaves in her wake.

Wounded Butterfly

Everything can change in a day. Friends can become enemies. Enemies can become friends. Sometimes a person will say something behind your back they don't have the courage to say to your face. Life is a balance between what is worth burdening your heart and what isn't. When you have moved past that part of your journey, just keep moving forward and don't look back. Letting go is always the best way of freeing yourself from things that just don't matter anymore. Break the chains that bind you.

°. ✳ .°

I loved you with so much passion. You loved me with so much destruction. Yet I still yearn for you.

Wounded Butterfly

There is an African proverb, "The ax forgets, but the tree remembers." Heartbreak is much like this. The person who caused us pain may forget but our heart remembers. Sometimes it remembers longer than we want it to. Healing is a process of going forward and at times going backward. It is not until we accept the loss and forgive that true healing begins. It is the truest measure of a beautiful soul; to forgive what is unforgivable and to rise above the pain. To shine your brightest even in the darkest moment of your heart.

Wounded Butterfly

Break the chains that bind you to the sorrows of your
yesterdays. Believe in the happiness and the promise of your
tomorrows. Always remember, stay true to yourself and
follow your path. Those that truly love you will be there to
catch you when you fall. Most importantly, they will always
be there to gently guide you, most of all.

°. ✳ .°

Those of us who have known darkness no longer fear the
monsters in the dark. The walls we build around us are to
keep the monsters in the light out. Those are the scariest of
them all.

Wounded Butterfly

Every day she paints on a new mask. Trying to hide what she does not want the world to see. A heart broken and battered by love and life. Eyes that have seen torment and pain. Only if she could know, she also hides her beautiful soul.

My heart lies on the floor in a hundred pieces. A puzzle of broken memories that no longer fit together. Each time I try to remember how we once were, the pieces break a little more.

Wounded Butterfly

You tell me I don't have wounds because I do not bleed. You tell me I don't have scars because you don't see them. You tell me I don't know pain because I don't cry. You tell me I am not screaming because you can't hear me. Then tell me, what does silence sound like? Tell me what broken looks like. Tell me what pain looks like. Tell me.

°• ✳ •°

I have never been afraid of being alone. When I am alone, I don't have to pretend, I can just be me.

You can't save someone who is drowning if you are the one who threw them in the water.

°• ❃ •°

I can feel your heart breaking.

The sadness in your soul.

The uncried tears you so bravely try to hide.

The silence in your words.

The emptiness in your voice.

Yes, I can feel your pain

because I walk with you in my pain.

Wounded Butterfly

———————

My heart weeps, longing to be reminded of who I once was

because I need to know.

The voices in my head tell me I will never be enough

That I will never measure up.

That love is not to be mine

That the sun will never shine its love on me

That the darkness will never set me free

I just need to know who I once was

and who I am meant to be.

°● ✳ ●°

Every breath I took loving you, I could slowly hear my heart

breaking.

Wounded Butterfly

The face of loneliness does not always look sad. The eyes do not always show pain, but if you listen in the silence, you can hear the heart breaking and the soul crying.

°• ✳ •°

Sadly sometimes you have to burn that bridge completely to the ground; Just to make sure that the person who caused you to burn it down in the first place finally realizes, they have no chance of it being rebuilt ever again.

Wounded Butterfly

I am but another tormented soul lost in the darkness waiting for the light to guide me home.

°• ✳ •°

I often wonder how tears can be so weightless but carry so much pain. A heart that can feel so much sadness but still feel love. A soul that feels so lost in darkness can always find the light. A butterfly can be wounded and still long to fly.

°• ✳ •°

Can you see the darkness swallowing me up? Wrapping his arms around me like a lover in the daylight.

Wounded Butterfly

Each of us has the capacity to love. It is within us to believe in ourselves. That is where the true understanding of love begins.

°● ✻ ●°

There are some sounds that hurt you, but there is only one sound that can break your heart. The saddest sound ever; the crack in someone's voice when they are on the verge of crying.

°● ✻ ●°

He said to the sculptor, "How can you make her understand my pain? She only sees what the world sees." At that moment he pierced my heart and I knew he understood.

Wounded Butterfly

Be careful of the ones who have honey dripping from their lips when they speak. Remember, even Snow White was fooled by the pretty poison apple.

°• ✳ •°

I saw a crow sitting on a gravestone. Just sitting there looking off in the distance, as if it was waiting for something or someone. I wondered if it was a sign of death or a sign of transition. Does it represent the soul of my ancestors or was it just an illusion?

°• ✳ •°

After dancing in the darkness for so long, I have finally learned how to dance in the light.

Wounded Butterfly

There were always hushed rumors about the dark angel who passed their way. He would leave destruction in his wake. No-one knew his name or who he was. But you always knew when he had been there; he always left broken souls and their remains lying in decay.

°• ✳ •°

I asked my heart today, "Why are you always so sad?" Softly in barely a whisper, it said, "Why do I always get broken?" I quietly turned and walked away.

Wounded Butterfly

Hell lives inside of me. It is the Devil's playhouse. He brings his demons with him to keep me company while he torments the darkness. Do not enter if you are afraid to play.

°. ✳ .°

Love murdered me, and you were the perfect weapon.

°. ✳ .°

There are nights I drown in my own tears.

Wounded Butterfly

As I sit here looking at the oncoming night sky, I wonder;

How many days of my life have I let pass me by?

Days holding on to regrets.

Days holding on to past hurts.

Days holding on to things I should have let go of a long time ago.

Days of staying in the darkness instead of walking into the light.

Now as I look at the days I have left, with a heart full of scars and a soul too heavy to carry. I will live until I can't.

Wounded Butterfly

Somehow, we must learn how to endure the pain we feel, to reach down deep within us and find the strength.

°● ❋ ●°

Those who are afraid to let you fly will try to keep you grounded and down on your knees. Don't let them clip your wings, keep reaching for the sky. Fly, fly, fly.

°● ❋ ●°

Sometimes a love story that starts out with "Once Upon a Time," is really a horror story in disguise.

Wounded Butterfly

When you are afraid of change, you will always need a safety net. Let go of your fears and fly, you can't grow if you don't try.

°• ✳ •°

I was like a frightened bird locked inside of a cage, too afraid to spread my wings and fly. Then one day you forgot to lock the door, and I spread my wings and that was the day I was born.

°• ✳ •°

You wrote our story as the victim. Then why am I the one with all the scars?

Wounded Butterfly

Don't let the seeds of doubt grow deep roots. You and you alone, control your journey. Be your own light and always "Shine On & Shine Bright."

°. ❋ .°

If you could have seen yourself through my eyes, I wonder if it would have made a difference?

°. ❋ .°

And just like that, her heart died again.

I am just another lost angel with a broken heart. There is nothing left of me now but brokenness as I sit here alone in the dark.

°• ❃ •°

You can kill me a thousand times and I will still live a thousand lives. Just to survive you.

°• ❃ •°

I walked through the darkest of nights expecting you to be waiting in the light. Little did I realize, you only wanted to keep me there. It was only in the darkness that you loved me. My light was just too much for you to bear.

Wounded Butterfly

There are some things that are more painful in silence. Silent tears are the loudest. Suffering heartache in silence when wearing a smile. But the most devastating is looking for an answer and receiving nothing but silence. Then realizing, sometimes the silence is the answer.

°• ✳ •°

I have pretended so long that I felt nothing. Then the surge of pain was so overwhelming that I knew if I did not purge it soon, I would be lost forever.

Wounded Butterfly

I was like a prizefighter always fighting for your love. In the end, I was always the loser.

My tears are not about you. They are about all the pain I have endured because of you. But don't let my tears lessen the message I am giving - "You broke my heart, but you did not break me."

Wounded Butterfly

As I look through the tear-stained pages of my memory. I wonder, how does a love story begin with so much promise, end with so much tragedy?

°● ✳ ●°

Our home is no longer a castle. Our love is a broken fairytale. You left me alone crying in the dark. Did you think I had an unbreakable heart?

°● ✳ ●°

It's funny to hear someone say, "I wish I were dead." When all I ever say is, "I wish I were alive.

Wounded Butterfly

I believe we all have moments in our lives we feel like the young Jenny Curran in the movie Forrest Gump.

"Dear God, make me a bird. So, I can fly far, far, far away from here."

We pray for release from a dark place or moment in time. When we need to believe in the strength of our wings so we can fly away. We pray that just for a moment we can be free from the darkness that haunts us.

Wounded Butterfly

These are the moments you must take a leap of faith. Trust in yourself or someone you love to show you the direction out of the dark. It is in our darkest moments we must continue to believe in our own light. We must believe we can get through this moment, believe everything is possible. Most importantly, we must always, "Believe in Ourselves."

°• ❋ •°

It doesn't always show its true colors in the light. Beware of the darkness that lurks within.

149

Wounded Butterfly

———————

We always think we have time,

But What is time?

Mere seconds that turn into minutes.

Minutes that turn into hours.

Hours that turn into days.

Days that turn into months.

Months that turn into years.

Years wasted because of our fears.

Then we have no more time.

°• ✳ •°

I can hear the soft crying as it drifts through the whispering
pines.

Wounded Butterfly

Is there an art to drowning? If there is, then I am a masterpiece - because I have been drowning for years.

°• ✳ •°

She had lost herself a long time ago. She knew there was no escaping from the weight of the darkness inside.

°• ✳ •°

For a moment I was a little girl again, picking up seashells on the beach. Not a care in the world. Just for a moment, I remembered who I was before life grabbed me.

Wounded Butterfly

When I was a little girl, I dreamt of traveling the world, seeing exotic places and becoming a famous poet writing about love and fairy tales. Although my dream did not come true, I'm still that little girl at heart, just with an old soul whose veins bleed ink, who writes about life in the real world.

°• ✳ •°

I was just a girl who pursued a fairytale and happened upon a nightmare.

Wounded Butterfly

Love is a type of murder. To survive it, you end up killing your mind.

°• ✳ •°

I remember you. I am the "you" who believed in fairy tales. When all the world was your kingdom. The little girl with wings who knew she could fly. I remember you, now it is time that you do.

°• ✳ •°

I have grown weary. My journey has been long, I'm finally down on my knees. Take me home.

Wounded Butterfly

I wonder if I look as empty as I feel. A sad soul of a girl trying to survive in a world that devours the weak - where evil touches goodness and breaks a heart. Maybe one day when the war is over, I will be the beautiful butterfly I once was

°• ✳ •°

She was the quietest one in the room. The one that no-one ever noticed.

°• ✳ •°

The bitter taste of yesterday continues to invade the sweetness of my today.

Wounded Butterfly

There are parts of me that wander alone, seeking the pieces of me that I lost along the way.

°• ✳ •°

There is an aching in my soul like a black wound that will never heal.

°• ✳ •°

My heart is a desolate place. It beats a steady rhythm of melancholy.

°• ✳ •°

There are times I feel so empty that even my heart wants to stop beating.

Wounded Butterfly

My heart has died from an overdose of feelings.

°• ✳ •°

As my wings continued to unfold, you would try to find new ways to stop me from flying.

°• ✳ •°

I have drowned a million times and you let me a million times.

°• ✳ •°

In the end, all of your promises were just words meant to destroy me.

Wounded Butterfly

Nobody knows the battles you have fought, the demons you have slain, the darkness you have overcome to get where you are today. They do not see the sadness behind your eyes, the scars that cannot be seen.

Hold your head high. Stay strong and be true to who you are. Be the Warrior, you are meant to be.

Wounded Butterfly

Epilogue

I learned a long time ago; people will always run from the truth but will stay for a lie. People will judge you based on another's opinion. There are always two sides to the same story. Moving on doesn't always mean moving forward. Most importantly, not everyone has good intentions and will always find a way to hurt you, even after the end of the relationship.

But remember, you control how you react. You are allowed to live your life and your truth. You don't have to apologize for who you are and your choices. Your worth is not determined by others but by you. Those who love you will always stand with you because they know what love you hold within your heart. Even in the midst of darkness, your soul shines brighter even when you are silent.

~ Mags

"Close some doors today. Not because of pride, incapacity or arrogance, but simply because they lead you nowhere."

~ Paulo Coelho

About the Author Margie Watts

Margie grew up in the Eastern Coastal area part of Georgia known as the Golden Isles. She loved it there, living near the ocean. Even as a child she loved looking out past the horizon. It felt like looking at forever. Walking, sand between her toes and picking up seashells. Just her and her shadow. Me time.

Butterflies were another of her favorites. Their beauty as they flew around. How they start out in the darkness of a cocoon and find their way out into the light as a beautiful butterfly. A reminder that darkness is not always a bad thing. There can be beauty from the darkness.

She was always an avid reader and always loved the spiritual meaning of the butterfly.

Butterflies are deep and powerful representations of life. Many cultures associate the butterfly with our souls. The Christian religion sees the butterfly as a symbol of resurrection. Around the world, people view the butterfly as representing endurance, change, hope, and life.

Always the constant dreamer, she never dreamed that all the tidbits on scraps of paper, notebooks filled with writings, would lead her to her dream of becoming an Author.

Dreams actually do come true.
Never give up.

Author's Note

If you or someone you know is a victim of emotional or physical abuse, you are not alone. Please reach out to someone for help. There is always hope.

From one survivor to another, yes you are a survivor, step into the light.

National Domestic Abuse Hotline

1-800-799-7233

1-800-787-3224 (TTY)

En Español

https://www.thehotline.org/

Disclosure: The National Domestic Abuse Hotline has not endorsed or agreed with any content or material in this book.